PHYSICS
in Your Everyday Life

PHYSICS
in Your Everyday Life

REAL WORLD SCIENCE

Enslow Publishing
101 W. 23rd Street
Suite 240
New York, NY 10011
USA
enslow.com

Richard Gaughan

Pour Sophie; merci de faire partie de ma vie.
Thanks to Cline Library for access to information and the tools to present it.

Published in 2020 by Enslow Publishing, LLC
101 W. 23rd Street, Suite 240, New York, NY 10011

Copyright © 2020 by Enslow Publishing, LLC.

All rights reserved.

No part of this book may be reproduced by any means without the written permission of the publisher.

Library of Congress Cataloging-in-Publication Data

Names: Gaughan, Richard, author.
Title: Physics in your everyday life / Richard Gaughan.
Description: New York, NY : Enslow Publishing, 2020. | Series: Real world science | Includes bibliographical references and index. | Audience: 5 to 8.
Identifiers: LCCN 2018054460| ISBN 9781978507616 (library bound) | ISBN 9781978509535 (pbk.)
Subjects: LCSH: Physics—Juvenile literature.
Classification: LCC QC25 .G38 2020 | DDC 530.078—dc23
LC record available at https://lccn.loc.gov/2018054460

Printed in the United States of America

To Our Readers: We have done our best to make sure all website addresses in this book were active and appropriate when we went to press. However, the author and the publisher have no control over and assume no liability for the material available on those websites or on any websites they may link to. Any comments or suggestions can be sent by email to customerservice@enslow.com.

Photo Credits: Cover, p. 3 herjua/Shutterstock.com; cover, p. 3 (science icons), back cover pattern kotoffei/Shutterstock.com; cover, p. 3 (globe graphic) Elkersh/Shutterstock.com; cover, interior pages (circular pattern) John_Dakapu/Shutterstock.com; p. 7 arka38/Shutterstock.com; p. 10 MidoSemsem/Shutterstock.com; p. 12 Imagno/Hulton Fine Art Collection/Getty Images; pp. 15, 23, 31, 38, 47, 56 Samuel Navarro-Meza; p. 18 © iStockphoto.com/omgimages; p. 20 Peter Baxter/Shutterstock.com; p. 26 Nasky/Shutterstock.com; pp. 28, 37, 45 Designua/Shutterstock.com; p. 35 PrinceOfLove/Shutterstock.com; p. 41 BSIP/Universal Images Group/Getty Images; p. 43 Belozersky/Shutterstock.com; pp. 52, 55 VectorMine/Shutterstock.com.

Contents

Introduction **6**

■ **Chapter 1**
The Rules of the World **9**

■ **Chapter 2**
Learning from Motion **17**

■ **Chapter 3**
Gases, Liquids, and Solids **25**

■ **Chapter 4**
Sound **33**

■ **Chapter 5**
Light **40**

■ **Chapter 6**
Electricity and Magnetism **49**

Afterword **58**

    Chapter Notes 59

    Glossary 60

    Further Reading 62

    Index 63

Introduction

All scientists have one goal: to build a mental model that explains how the world works. That's a job with a few important parts. First, scientists observe the physical world. Second, they come up with rules that describe what they see. Third, they test their rules. Then they go back to the first step. It's a tricky job because the world is complicated.

Think about dropping a feather from your hand, over and over. Every time, the feather drops a little differently and lands in a new spot. The motion is complicated. Scientists take complicated things and split them into separate simpler things.

One way to split things is to concentrate on one type of question at a time. Questions about living things—plants, animals, insects, and microscopic organisms—are studied by biologists. Questions about how atoms and molecules combine and break apart are studied by chemists. Questions about energy and matter are studied by physicists.

Chemistry and biology are also about energy and matter. A cow eating grass is a living organism, so this is something biologists study. Grass in a cow's stomachs is broken apart by the action of acids and enzymes, which is chemistry. But those activities are interactions of energy and matter. So biology and chemistry are just special ways of studying complicated physics.

That's why physics is important. Everything that happens depends upon matter and energy—everything from trees blowing in the breeze to stars exploding.

The rules of physics in everyday life are the same as the rules of physics everywhere. The things you observe in your house or

Introduction

The motion of a feather is difficult to predict. This is because its motion is described by many different rules working at the same time.

Physics in Your Everyday Life

at the playground will help you understand things that happen under the ocean, inside Earth, and out in space.

To understand physics in daily life, we must understand the two ways physicists approach any question.

One part is everything that is already known. That is, what is the current mental model for how the world works? Another part is the current observation. That is, what is the new evidence? The two parts go together: a mental model is the result of previous observations, and new observations can change the mental model.

Every time an observation is made, scientists need to figure out if it fits in with the existing mental model or if the mental model needs to change. When a mental model agrees with many observations, it is called a theory. It's important to realize that when observations *don't* fit with a mental model, then the theory must be wrong. That's another way of saying that evidence is always more important than theory.

Now you're ready to investigate the physics of everyday life.

The Rules of the World

Chapter 1

Imagine you hold a feather. Drop it. Drop it again. And again. As the feather falls, it twirls, flips, and glides. It is almost impossible to get the feather to fall the same way, take the same amount of time to hit the ground, or even land in precisely the same spot.

What determines where the feather lands? As with many everyday events, that's a tough question. There are two ways to think about it. First, you could say, "The feather's just going to fall however it wants to." Second, you can say, "The feather falls in a very complicated way because lots of separate things affect it."

Scientists don't say that the feather just falls the way it wants to, because that would mean that there were no rules. There's one thing every scientist can agree upon: the physical world works according to rules. A scientist would look at that falling feather and realize that many different things must be affecting it—the tough job is figuring out which things.

Searching for the Rules

How did people in the ancient world, such as the philosopher Aristotle (c. 384–322 BCE), try to discover rules that describe how things move?

Aristotle tried to answer by thinking about the problem. Feathers and balls, for example, move in different ways, he figured, so it makes sense they work by different rules. Feathers flit and twirl, balls roll and bounce. If you throw a feather or a ball, it moves because whatever it is in contact with (the air or the ground) pushes it along in its own particular fashion. That was more or less Aristotle's explanation of how things move.

Physics in Your Everyday Life

Aristotle tried to explain the world by thinking about how things *should* be, according to his own ideas. Today's science starts by trying to describe how things *are*, based on observations.

The Rules of the World

That worked for a long time, but then people thought about a different kind of question.

Imagine that every day you walk by a fist-sized rock in the middle of a field. Would you ever expect that rock to jump up and fly away? No, rocks don't do that. But what if you picked up the rock and heaved it? In that case, the rock would jump up and fly away. The rock is still a rock, so it should still behave like a rock, but you made it behave like a sparrow, flying through the air.

About eight hundred years after Aristotle, John Philoponus (c. 490–570 CE) thought about things like that rock you sent flying. Philoponus said that the rock could move because a person gave it something he called "impetus." The rock moves until the impetus it was given runs out; then it falls.[1]

That's a better explanation, but it still has problems. When you throw the rock, it will stop when it hits the ground. But what if you threw the rock over the edge of the cliff? Would you expect it to run out of "impetus" and stop level with the ground at your feet? That is, would you expect the ball to hang there in midair because it had run out of juice?

Of course not. It keeps falling. But it couldn't keep falling if Philoponus was right. For the next one thousand years, other people added more to the understanding. Finally, somebody came up with a powerful and accurate explanation. Isaac Newton (1643–1727) realized that a body would *change its motion* only if a force was acting on it.

As Newton explained, when you change the rock's motion—from not moving to flying up—you push it with a force. If it doesn't keep flying in the same direction, then some other force is acting on it. Does the rock keep flying up forever? No. It falls to the ground.

What force is acting on that rock? That would be the force of gravity. That's the attraction that any body exerts on any other body. In our everyday experience, we can think of this as the force

Physics in Your Everyday Life

Isaac Newton observed objects falling on Earth and the motion of the moon and planets. His observations led him to come up with a mathematical description of the way the world works. This showed that the universe works according to the same rules, on Earth and everywhere in space.

The Rules of the World

Newton's Laws

Scientific laws are shortcuts—little hints that help us understand more complicated theories. Isaac Newton came up with three rules we now call Newton's laws of motion:

■ **1.** An object will not change the way it is moving unless a force acts on it.

■ **2.** An object will speed up, slow down, or change direction only if there is a force, and a bigger force makes a bigger change.

■ **3.** For each force in one direction, there is an equal force in the opposite direction.

pulling objects toward the center of Earth. That force always acts on every object on Earth.

Testing the Rules

Just by *thinking* about rocks moving, you were able to decide that certain rules didn't work and that some other theory was better. But how did you make that decision? For example, if you threw a rock off a cliff and it really did stop in midair, then maybe impetus really would explain motion. You know, though, that a rock will not hang in midair because you have tossed things up and seen them fall, and you've *never* seen one stop before it hit the ground. You didn't have to test that idea because you have already tested it.

Physics in Your Everyday Life

If you were testing something you hadn't seen, you wouldn't just sit and think. You would think about what you expect, then you would do the test and see if you were right. That kind of test is called an experiment. The idea of an experiment is pretty new. Neither Aristotle nor John Philoponus would have thought of doing that. Nowadays we know the only way to *really* test an idea is to do an experiment.

Activity: Rules of Motion

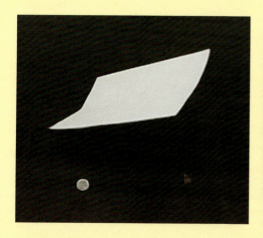

The flat paper and the crumpled paper both fall from the same height, through the same air, but their motion is very different.

Things You Will Need:

- a piece of paper
- a coin

■ **1.** Hold one piece of paper about 3 feet (about a meter) off the floor.

■ **2.** Drop it.

■ **3.** Pick up the paper and put the coin on the floor right where the paper dropped.

■ **4.** Drop the paper again from the same spot and the same height. Can you hit the coin?

■ **5.** Crumple the paper into as tight a ball as you can make.

Physics in Your Everyday Life

■ **6.** Hold the crumpled paper ball about 3 feet above the floor, then drop it.

■ **7.** Put the coin where the paper hit the floor. Can you drop the ball from the same spot and the same height and hit the coin? What does that mean?

The flat sheet of paper interacts with air in a complicated way. When you crumple the paper you reduce that interaction. By crumpling the paper, you are saying something like, "I know air can mess up the way a piece of paper falls, so I will make a less complicated experiment." Scientists do that all the time. They design controlled experiments to make sure they are studying just one thing at a time, saving the other things for another experiment.

If you can consistently hit the same spot with the crumpled up paper, then you know there is some rule that describes how things fall—even if it's sometimes complicated!

Learning from Motion

Chapter 2

Scientists have discovered that the universe works according to rules. If Jay does an experiment on his kitchen table and Sally does the exact same experiment, they will both get the same results. But it's more significant than that.

A truth Jay discovers on his table will be true at the bottom of the ocean, the top of Mount Everest, or in the middle of the sun. All of those places might be more complicated—just like a falling feather is more complex than a falling baseball—but the same rules work everywhere. What you learn at your kitchen table can help you understand events throughout the universe.

Forces in Balance

Newton's laws of motion say that an object changes its motion if a force is acting on it. Put another way, if an object *does not* change its motion, then no force is acting on it. That's not exactly true because the force Newton talked about was not just one force; it was the total of all the forces. That's called the net force.

Imagine a heavy rope stretched across a room. Emilio and Janet pick it up and pull it so they can reel it in to one loop. The motion of the rope changes from lying on the floor to moving across the room. Because the motion changes, we know they are applying a force to the rope.

What if Francesca and Timothy are pulling just as hard on the other end of the rope? Emilio and Janet are still pulling, but now the rope isn't moving. Emilio and Janet are putting a force on the rope, but it is perfectly balanced by the force with which Francesca

Physics in Your Everyday Life

The middle of this rope is not moving, but there's a lot of force on it. Why doesn't it move? Each team is pulling very hard, but their forces are perfectly balanced. The rope doesn't move until one team pulls harder than the other.

and Timothy are pulling. The rope isn't moving, therefore the forces are in balance. That doesn't tell how hard everyone is pulling, just that the force in one direction balances the force in the opposite direction.

You see forces in balance all the time. If you let go of a ball 3 feet (1 meter) above the ground, you would expect it to drop.

Learning from Motion

That is, you would expect it to speed up in the downward direction, which means Earth's gravitational attraction pulls it downward.

What if you let the ball go, but you rested it on a table? The ball is still the same distance above the floor, it still is affected by Earth's gravitational pull, but it's not moving. Has gravity disappeared? No, the table is pushing up on the ball just as hard as gravity is pulling down. The forces are in balance.

Scientists have a fancy name for forces in balance; it's called equilibrium.

Think about that ball a little more. Hang it on a string from the ceiling. If you tap the ball and move it away from the bottom center, it will swing up, then come back to the center. That is stable equilibrium. If you push it away from where the forces are in balance, it will come back to that spot. (Unstable equilibrium also has everything in balance, but a small change will knock things away from balance. A coin on its edge is an example of unstable equilibrium.)

Here are a couple more things about the ball on the string. First, no matter which direction you push the ball, the forces will try to push it back to where it started from. That's called a restoring force because it works to return things to the way they were. Restoring forces show up in many different places—from the middle of the sun to your bathtub.

Second, when you release the ball from a high point, it doesn't just return to the bottom. The string will get vertical and shoot past, swinging up the other side. It will keep going back and forth for a long time. That kind of back-and-forth motion has a special name. It's called simple harmonic motion, and it also appears in many places—from the concert hall to the beach.

Physics in Your Everyday Life

If this ball were not tied to a rope, when you hit it, it would fly away. The string pulls it back to the pole in the center. That's a type of restoring force: you try to push the ball away, and the string pulls it back.

Learning from Motion

Energy

You probably hear the word "energy" many times a day. Physicists have a special meaning for energy. When your mom reminds you to do your homework, you might say, "I'll do it later; I don't have much energy." What you mean is that you don't feel like doing anything.

Physicists talk about two different kinds of energy. The easiest one to understand is the energy of motion, called kinetic energy. If two objects have the same mass—if they "weigh the same"—then the one going faster has more energy. (Weight is not absolutely the same as mass, but it's close enough to think of it that way for everyday situations.) If two objects have the same speed, then the heavier one has more energy.

The Change in Energy

A rock on a cliff has zero kinetic energy but a lot of potential energy due to its height. When it falls, right before it reaches ground level, its kinetic energy is largest and its potential energy is smallest.

If the rock were dropped from an airplane, it would already be moving as it passed the cliff top–its kinetic energy at that point would not be zero. But it would gain just as much kinetic energy as it fell to the ground.

The change in potential energy is always equal and opposite to the change in kinetic energy.

Physics in Your Everyday Life

The other type is called potential energy, and it is essentially the energy of position. That is, it's the energy an object has because of where it is.[1] For example, if you hold the ball on the string farther away from vertical, it will have more energy just because of where it is when you release it.

One of the most important discoveries of physics is that energy cannot be created or destroyed, just converted from one type to another. That's the law of conservation of energy, and it is true for everything humans have ever observed.

Activity: Energy in Simple Harmonic Motion

When released down the side of the bowl, the ball travels up the opposite side. The restoring force pulls the ball down to the center, but it travels back and forth until it transfers energy away.

Things You Will Need:

- a marble or other solid ball
- a large soup bowl or a mixing bowl

Physics in Your Everyday Life

■ **1.** Put the ball in the bowl. The ball rests where forces are balanced.

■ **2.** Move the ball a little bit up the side of the bowl. Hold the ball still, then release it. Does the ball go back to the equilibrium point? Then what?

■ **3.** Do the same thing with the ball a little higher up the side of the bowl. How fast does the ball move through the equilibrium point? How high does the ball move up the opposite side?

■ **4.** Put a few tablespoons of water in the bowl and repeat the experiment. What is different about the way the ball moves?

When the ball is displaced from the equilibrium point, then released, it travels through the equilibrium point and keeps going up the other side. But it can't go higher than the height at which it was first released.

When you release the ball from a higher starting position, you are giving it more potential energy, which means it should have more kinetic energy as it passes through the equilibrium point.

When you put some water in the bottom, some of the ball's energy goes into moving the water, so the ball will come to a stop much earlier.

Gases, Liquids, and Solids

Chapter 3

You now know the rules of physics you discover on your kitchen table are the same you would find if you were at the bottom of the ocean or at the top of a mountain. The same thing is true as objects get even smaller. For example, scientists know that matter is composed of tiny particles called atoms and molecules. Atoms are extremely tiny balls made of a cloud of very light electrons zipping around a much heavier center. The center is called a nucleus, and it is made up of particles called protons and neutrons. To get an idea of the size of an atom, imagine you were so big that your fingertip is as wide as the distance between Los Angeles and Chicago. If your finger were that big, one atom would be as large as a Ping-Pong ball.

You can think of those tiny particles as microscopic marbles, and the rules you discover on your kitchen table apply to those atoms and molecules, too. Things are more complicated when you look at only one or two microscopic particles at a time, but everything we can see is made of many millions of atoms, so we'll ignore those complications.

Atoms and Molecules

The back and forth motion you saw in the bowl—the simple harmonic motion—happens in many other situations. Simple harmonic motion also happens if you connect two marbles together with a spring. With no extra force, the marbles sit separated by an equilibrium distance. If the marbles get closer,

Physics in Your Everyday Life

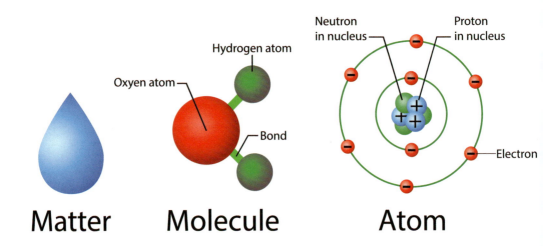

The structure of matter

Matter — Molecule — Atom

Atoms and molecules act a lot like marbles connected together with springs. The parts of an atom are protons, neutrons, and electrons. Meanwhile, molecules themselves are atoms connected together with spring-like forces.

the spring will move them apart. If the marbles are moved farther apart, the spring will bring them together.

For marbles sitting on a table not moving, there is no net force. Let's imagine you put up some cardboard walls around the edges of the flat table. With just one pair of marbles sitting still in the middle of the table, nothing would bump against those cardboard walls.

Now make a few changes. Add more pairs of marbles. And instead of having them sitting still, have them rolling around a bit. As they roll, they will bump into each other now and then. When

Gases, Liquids, and Solids

they bump, they can send each other spinning, vibrating back and forth, or dashing across the table. At any instant, the table is covered by little pairs of dancing marbles. They bounce against each other and against the walls.

Imagine you can measure the force hitting against the walls. The total force on a wall is just the sum of all the forces from each of the marble pairs that crash against the wall. More crashes or harder crashes create a bigger force on the wall.

How could you make more crashes, or harder crashes, or both? What if you put more pairs of marbles on the table? What if you sped up all the marbles? Both of those things would make a larger force against the wall.

The total force against any given area of the wall is called pressure. The pressure gets higher with more marbles or faster marbles. Now imagine you shrink those marbles until they're as small as grains of sand, then shrink them that much again, and again. Now you have an idea of what a gas looks like.

Think about putting a new tire on a bicycle. The inner tube starts out soft and floppy. You can easily squeeze it because there is not much pressure pushing against you. But when you add more air—just like putting more marbles on the table—the pressure goes up. The more air, the higher the pressure, and the harder the tire becomes.

Liquids and Solids

Gases, liquids, and solids are all made of atoms—something like those marbles on the table. So why do liquids and solids act differently than gases?

Start with that mental model of a gas—as pairs of marbles spinning and dashing about. Now add springs connecting different pairs of marbles together. These springs, though, are weaker. A

Physics in Your Everyday Life

STATE OF MATTER

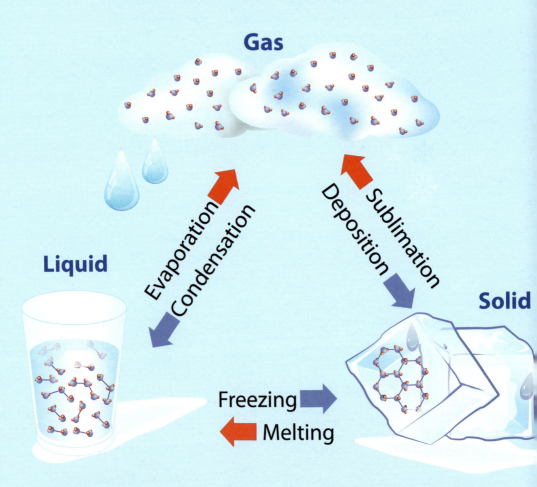

Molecules also connect to other molecules with spring-like forces. Depending upon how strongly those spring-like forces are acting, a material will be either a solid, liquid, or gas.

Gases, Liquids, and Solids

pair of marbles moving fast enough can break the connections. That pair roams the table, but now it's carrying a loose broken spring end. When it gets close to another pair of marbles, the broken end latches on. So even though some pairs of marbles might be loose at any moment, it doesn't take long for them to join up again.

That's like a liquid. You can't squish the marbles closer to each other because those extra springs don't let them get too close. And the marbles move, but the springs don't let them stray completely away from their neighbors.

Temperature and Motion

If we get close to something hot, our nerves send us a signal: be careful! If you could see the individual atoms and molecules, you would be able to tell that heat is just a measure of movement. In a stone around a campfire, for example, the rock doesn't move as it heats up, but the individual atoms and molecules vibrate more strongly.

Just about every material can exist as a gas, a liquid, or a solid. Each material has its own unique set of springs with different strengths. Water, for example, has some spring connections that break if the temperature is greater than 32° Fahrenheit (0° Celsius). That changes it from a solid to a liquid. It has other connections that break at 212° Fahrenheit (100° Celsius), where it turns from a liquid to a gas.

Physics in Your Everyday Life

You can turn this into a solid by taking the "extra" *weak* springs and turning them into *strong* springs. When one of those marbles moves faster, it shakes back and forth, but the strong spring keeps it in pretty much the same place. If you add enough energy to the marble, it will shake enough that it makes its next-door neighbors move, too. Adding energy increases the motion a lot, but the marbles don't fly all over the place. They stay in the same spot, just vibrating back and forth more rapidly. That's a solid. You can see it will keep the same shape no matter how much each of the marbles is vibrating.

Now you understand gases, liquids, and solids because they follow the same rules as those marbles on your table.

Activity: Pressure and Temperature

The temperature of the water inside the jug affects the temperature of the air inside as well, which in turn changes the pressure.

Things You Will Need:

- an empty plastic milk or water jug, with the cap
- hot and cold tap water

Physics in Your Everyday Life

■ **1.** Put a half inch or so of hot water in the jug.

■ **2.** Put the top on and shake the bottle vigorously.

■ **3.** Put your hand against the side of the jug. What happens?

■ **4.** Pour the water out and put about the same amount of cold water in the jug.

■ **5.** Replace the cap and give the jug another shake. Put your hand against the side again. What happens?

When you put hot or cold water in the jug, you're changing the average temperature. When you shake the bottle, you mix hot or cold water with the air, making the air either warmer or colder.

Unlike in the bicycle tire, you aren't adding or subtracting air from the jug; you're taking the same amount of air and making the individual molecules move faster or slower. The sides of the bottle move out or in depending on the pressure, so you change the pressure by changing the temperature.

Sound

Chapter 4

As you know, physics studies the interaction of matter and energy. All the interactions we have looked at so far involve physically touching an object. Energy and matter, however, can also interact over long distances.

Imagine Sabrina and Felix are studying at different ends of a long table in the library. If Sabrina wants to get Felix's attention, she could poke him with a stick. Sabrina's hand would put a force on the stick and the stick would exert a force on Felix's shoulder. He would feel the force and look up to see Sabrina.

Sabrina has an easier way to get Felix's attention. She transmits energy through the air and exerts a force on him. That's just an unusual way of describing an everyday activity: Sabrina talks to Felix.

Moving Molecules and Atoms

You know atoms *can* connect to each other with a spring-like force, but they don't *have* to be connected. In air, for example, most of the atoms are connected in pairs, but the pairs aren't connected to one another. The pairs are air molecules. Molecules in a gas act pretty much like marbles on a table—or, even better, marbles on an ice skating rink. The rink is a good model for air because just like molecules in air, marbles only change speed and direction when they hit something, such as another marble or the side of the rink.

Imagine a rink with thousands of marbles flitting around. They're spaced so they can roll around a bit before they crash into

Physics in Your Everyday Life

each other. Now draw nine imaginary squares next to each other around a small part of the ice. Count the number of particles that move in and out of the middle square every minute. If there are a lot of particles in the middle square, there will be a lot of crashes that can send particles out of the area. But if there are just as many particles in the squares around that one, then just as many particles will be coming in.

What if the middle square has extra particles, though? A bunch of particles will be knocked out of the square, but fewer will come in. After a minute, the square will have fewer particles than it started with. What if the middle square started with fewer particles than its neighbors? Not as many particles leave as come in, so after a minute, the middle square gains particles.

If the squares have the same number of particles—the same density—then the number of particles will stay the same. If the number of particles starts higher, then it will go lower, while if it starts lower, it will get higher. Does that remind you of anything? It's a restoring force!

When the density is the same in all the squares, everything stays balanced—in equilibrium. When the density gets higher or lower, the particles will be pushed back toward equilibrium. As in other situations with a restoring force, the density overshoots the equilibrium point and then turns around in the opposite direction.

That's how a sound wave is created.

Sound Waves

To understand sound waves, we need one more bit of information: in a sound wave, the initial variation in density has a direction. For marbles on the ice, we just imagined that one square had extra marbles in it. In the real world, the higher density starts with something that disturbs the equilibrium.

Sound

Sound waves, shown here on a sound-editing program, are areas of high and low air pressure. The restoring force acts in a way that sends the regions of high and low pressure away from where the sound starts.

When you clap your hands, for example, you push air closer together until your hands meet and force all the air away. That initial variation in density starts where your hands meet. The density variation then moves away.

Measuring Waves

A piano key hits a string that vibrates at one single rate. The A string, for example, vibrates with a frequency of 440 times per second, also called 440 Hertz (Hz).

If you could see each molecule, you would see the regions of high and low pressure. Those regions would look like shells spreading out from the piano. The distance from one region of high density to the next region is the wavelength.[1]

Waves have one more important property: they move at a certain speed. The speed is equal to the wavelength times the frequency. For air, the speed is about 750 miles per hour (about 335 meters per second).[2]

Remember that a higher density means a higher force—a higher pressure. When you talk or sing, small folds of flesh in your throat vibrate back and forth very quickly. As they do, they disturb the equilibrium density and the regions of high and low density travel outward from your mouth. That's called a pressure wave.

When those variations in density hit any surface, they'll push against that surface at the same rate of the initial vibrations.

Sound

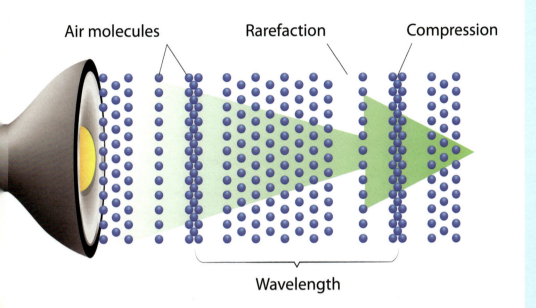

If you could see each molecule of the air, this is what a sound wave would look like. The crowded molecules (compression) push each other more than the spread-out molecules (rarefaction). That makes a restoring force that pushes the wave through the air.

That is, if your vocal folds vibrate back and forth a thousand times a second, then the pressure wave pushes against any surface it hits at a frequency of a thousand times a second. If that surface happens to be in your friend's ear, your friend will hear a sound vibrating a thousand times a second.

That's how molecules and atoms carry energy in sound from one place to another.

Activity: Seeing Sound

You can "see" sound waves as ripples in this wineglass filled with water.

Things You Will Need:

- a wineglass
- a spoon
- a room with ceiling lights

38

Sound

■ **1.** Fill the wineglass about one-quarter full with water.

■ **2.** Set it in a spot where you can see the reflection of a ceiling light right in the middle.

■ **3.** Firmly hold down the base of the wineglass. Gently tap the side of the wineglass with the spoon as you look at the reflection of the ceiling light. What can you tell about the surface of the water?

The wineglass produces sound and also waves you can see in the water. The molecules in the wineglass have an equilibrium location—that's the normal shape of the glass. When you tap the side, you change the position of the sides just a little, but the restoring force brings it back. You know a restoring force makes simple harmonic motion—vibration back and forth. That vibration pushes against the air, which you can hear, and against the water, which you can see.

Light

Now we understand how sound can transmit energy. Sound disturbs equilibrium in the air. A restoring force works to restore equilibrium, but as it does, it pushes the disturbance farther away. The disturbance travels with a certain speed away from where it started, and it can transfer energy to another object—such as an ear—that is far away.

There's one more very important thing to realize. If you were to look at any one air molecule, you would see that it doesn't move very far as the wave moves. That is, the *energy* of the wave travels, but the atoms and molecules themselves do not move much.

In many ways, light travels in just the same way. But there are a few important differences. To understand those similarities and differences, we have to look a little more closely at atoms and molecules.

Atoms and Molecules: Springing Around

Molecules are something like marbles connected together with springs. Think about one pair of marbles connected together with one spring. If you were to hold one marble and let the other hang down, how would it behave if you tapped the lower marble? It would move up and down, but how quickly?

To answer that question, think about a playground swing. Let's say Shawna pushes Mahmoud as he sits on the swing. Shawna gives Mahmoud a little push. Let's say the swing goes back and forth one time every two seconds. If Shawna gives him a bigger push, he goes faster, but he travels farther before swinging back,

Light

This model of an atom shows a cloud of electrons surrounding the nucleus. The "springs" that hold the electrons to the nucleus vibrate at the same energy as light waves, so energy can transfer back and forth between atoms and light.

Physics in Your Everyday Life

so he will still make one round trip every two seconds. Because the swing makes one-half a round trip in one second, its frequency is one-half per second, or one-half Hz. That is called the natural frequency, or resonant frequency, of the swing.

If Shawna wants to help Mahmoud, would it do her any good to push once a second? No, because when she pushes a second time, the swing will be starting backward. Shawna should push every time the swing starts forward again. That is, she should push at the same rate as the swing is moving. Put another way, she should put energy into the swing at its resonant frequency.

The same thing is true for the marbles connected with the spring. The spring has one natural frequency. The pair of marbles will interact with the world best at that resonant frequency.

One more discussion about atoms and springs before we can get to light: atoms are connected to each other with a springlike force. Remember, though, atoms are something like a heavy dot surrounded by a bunch of light particles. Spring-like forces connect those light particles—the electrons—to the heavy nucleus. Those springs are different from the springs that connect atoms into molecules, and the resonant frequency is one of the differences. That is, the springs that connect different atoms have a different resonant frequency than the springs that hold the electrons to the nucleus.

One final reminder: any system—a swing, a pair of marbles, or an atom—trades energy with the rest of the world at its resonant frequency.

Atoms and Light

Let's say you heat up a bunch of atoms. Remember, that's pretty much like making a bunch of marbles move fast and crash into each other hard. Some of those crashes will start the atoms

Light

vibrating. Again, each marble is like a heavy dot connected with springs to some tiny dancing electrons. Each of those springs has a resonant frequency. So as the atoms heat up, all that crashing starts them vibrating at their resonant frequencies.

Those atoms, like other systems with a restoring force, would like to get back to their equilibrium position. If you start a swing moving, walk away, and come back five minutes later, it will be hanging straight down. Some of the swing's energy has gone into things like friction, sound, and movement of the air, leaving it in its equilibrium position.

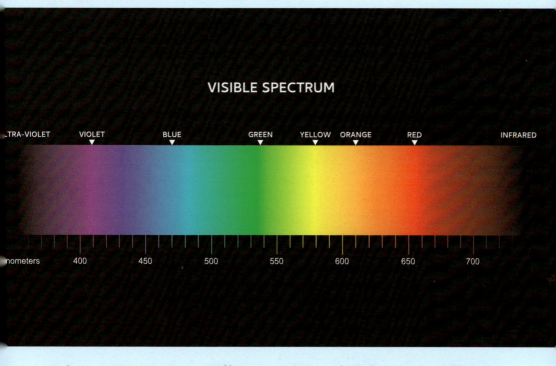

Light carries energy. Different colors of light carry different amounts of energy. Blue light has higher energy than red light, for example. Light interacts with atoms when the light's energy matches the energy of a particular atom's "springs."

Physics in Your Everyday Life

How Light Travels

Light carries energy. So does sound. The energy in a sound wave is carried in moving air molecules. Even though any one air molecule will only move back and forth a little, the energy travels.

What carries a light wave? It took physicists a long time to realize that light carries itself! When an atom or molecule releases a bundle of light energy, it creates a new kind of object. To balance out the creation of that new kind of object, another object is created, too. Those two objects are called electric fields and magnetic fields. When the electric field gets big, the magnetic field gets small, so energy trades between the electric and magnetic fields as light travels along.

The atoms also want to get to their equilibrium positions; they want to vibrate as little as possible. But there's no friction, sound, or air to take energy away. An atom can only vibrate less strongly if it releases a bundle of vibrating energy. That's what light is, a bundle of vibrating energy. Light of different colors is simply energy that vibrates at a different frequency.

The springs that hold electrons to the nucleus of an atom vibrate at the frequency of light. An atom that returns to its equilibrium position releases the bundle of energy as a bit of light.

That describes how light is emitted. It is absorbed and reflected more or less the same way.

So far we've talked only about single atoms and molecules built from only two atoms. Some molecules, however, are built

Light

from dozens, hundreds, or even thousands of atoms. Each type of molecule has its own set of springs. This means complicated molecules can have many resonant frequencies.

When a bundle of light meets a molecule, the interaction depends upon the match between the resonant frequency of the molecule and the resonant frequency of the light. Three things can happen:

- 1. The molecule can absorb the light.
- 2. The molecule can reflect the light.
- 3. The light can pass right by.

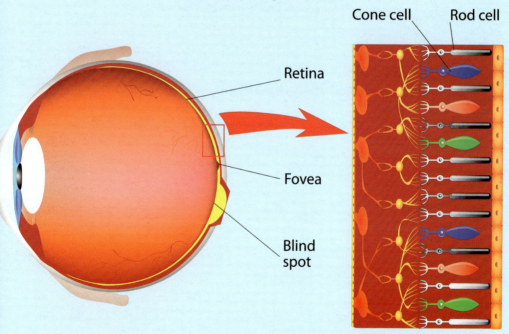

The retina of the human eye contains different photoreceptor cells, including cone cells. Each cone cell has different light-absorbing molecules that make it sensitive to blue, red, or green wavelengths.

Physics in Your Everyday Life

For example, dark ink looks dark because the ink molecules absorb the light while the paper molecules reflect it. Your eyes work the same way. In the back of your eye, three different types of molecules absorb light energy. Each of the three types of molecules has its own unique set of springs.

You know now that means each type of molecule has its own particular resonant frequency. In your eye, one type vibrates at the frequency of red light, one at the frequency of green light, and one at the frequency of blue light. When light of the right color hits those molecules, they absorb energy and send a signal to your brain. That's pretty complicated stuff, but it all starts with an understanding of marbles on a tabletop.

Activity: Resonant Frequency of Light

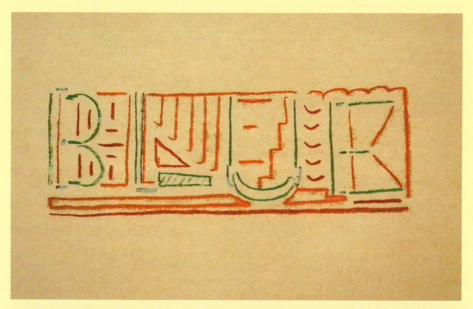

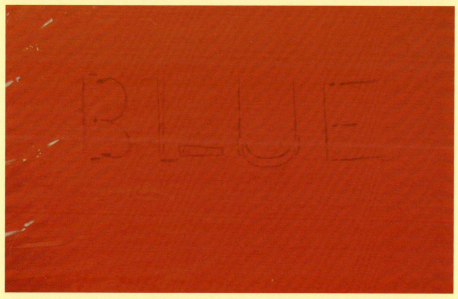

If you put red cellophane over red writing, the writing becomes invisible!

47

Physics in Your Everyday Life

Things You Will Need:

- a colored pen, crayon, or pencil
- white paper

- a translucent piece of plastic or cellophane the same color as the pen, pencil, or crayon

■ **1.** Look at the paper through the plastic. What color does it appear?

■ **2.** Write or draw something in the same color on the paper. Now look at it through the plastic. What do you see?

Light is made of many different colors. Each color is a different frequency. A red piece of plastic looks red because it absorbs all the resonant frequencies *other than* red. You can see red writing because the rest of the paper reflects all the colors, and the red ink reflects only red. The plastic, though, only lets red light through—even when the page is white! So all the spots look red, which means you can't see the writing!

Electricity and Magnetism

Chapter 6

A couple hundred years ago, there were no cell phones, computers, or cameras. Scientists wanted to learn about the world, but they didn't have the tools we take for granted today. They tried to explain the way the world worked in terms of things they could observe.

What could they observe? They could see objects of different colors. They could measure an object's size and weight. They could measure how long it took for an object to move from one spot to another.

They put their observations together to come up with some rules, such as Newton's second law of motion: an object will only change its motion if it is acted on by a net force. That gave them hope they could also understand some other mysterious observations.

Electric Charge

Have you ever walked across a carpeted floor and gotten shocked when you touch a metal doorknob? Or maybe you've rubbed a blown-up balloon on your shirt then had it stick against the wall. Those are effects of electric charge.

People had observed those kinds of effects for thousands of years, but it wasn't until they described things such as gravity that they realized it might be possible to describe strange effects such as electric shocks. This wasn't an easy thing to do, and here's why: gravity is invisible, but it works on every object you can touch. Gravity attracts everything people can see—feathers, bowling balls, cups of tea, etc. But electricity doesn't act like that.

49

Physics in Your Everyday Life

You rub a balloon on your shirt and it sticks to a wall. But if you rub a library book on your shirt, it won't stick on the wall. In fact, if you *don't* rub the balloon on your shirt, it won't stick on the wall either. The balloon appears to be exactly the same, but sometimes it sticks to the wall and sometimes it doesn't! There must be something about that balloon that changes, but the size is the same, the weight is the same, the color is the same—something invisible changes when you rub the balloon on your shirt.

Gravity is invisible, but it works on things that are visible. The electric force is invisible, but it acts on things that are invisible, too.

So how do you think they investigated these invisible things? They used what they already knew: if an object's motion changes, there is a net force on it.

They discovered that some objects react to the electric force after being rubbed with other objects.[1] For example, glass rubbed with silk will then react to an electric force. Amber (fossilized tree resin) rubbed with rabbit fur will also react to an electric force.

What does it mean to "react to an electric force"? Scientists learned the answer through observing various situations. For example, they could hang an object from a string and bring another object close to it. If the hanging object moved, then there was a force. If the hanging object didn't move, then there was no force. They made the following observations:

- **Unrubbed amber or glass does not move.**
- **Rubbed amber pushes rubbed amber away.**
- **Rubbed glass pushes rubbed glass away.**
- **Rubbed amber attracts rubbed glass.**
- **Rubbed glass attracts rubbed amber.**
- **Rabbit fur attracts the amber it rubbed.**
- **Silk attracts the glass it rubbed.**

Electricity and Magnetism

From observations like these, scientists realized that objects have weight, color, shininess, and things like that, but these objects can also have a new property. Observers called the new property "charge." They realized charge comes in two types: positive and negative. They found that charges of the same type repel one another. Charges of different types attract one another. They also found that two objects would push or pull one another more if they had more charge. Finally, they learned that the push or pull is weaker if the charges are moved farther apart.

Atoms and Springs

Earlier we learned that atoms have heavy centers surrounded by lighter particles. We pretended those light particles were connected to the heavy centers with tiny little springs. There aren't *really* tiny little springs inside atoms—there is something that *acts like* tiny springs.

The heavy nucleus at the center of an atom has *positively charged* particles called protons. The light particles that whirl around, the electrons, are *negatively charged*. The little "spring" we talked about is the electric force that attracts oppositely charged particles to one another.

Scientists didn't learn all that at once, of course. It took hundreds of years and thousands of experiments. There is still one big mystery about electric charge: *why* should rubbing a piece of amber with rabbit fur make electrons jump from one to the other?

Magnetism

Electricity is the name we give to the force that makes one charge move another. But it turns out that if charges move, they generate another force called magnetism. Magnetism is the force that attracts certain metals, especially any metal with iron in it.

Physics in Your Everyday Life

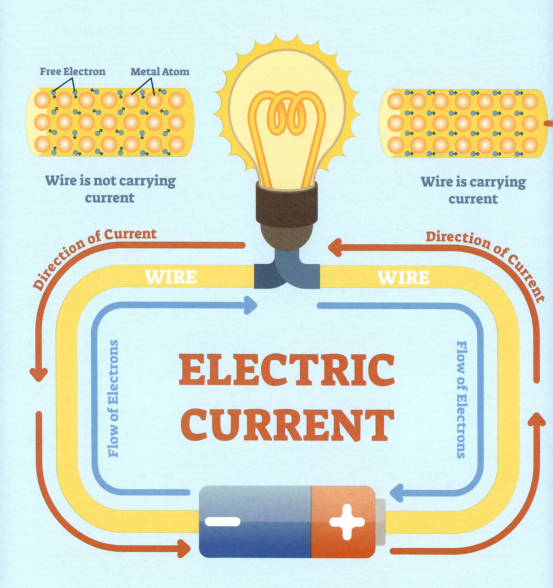

Thousands of experiments have come together to reveal the workings of electricity. Some electrons in a metal are only attached to their atoms with very weak springs. Electrical current happens when those electrons are pushed away from their home atoms.

Electricity and Magnetism

Moving charge has a special name; it's called electric current. If you put a current through a wire, you turn it into a magnet. If you wind a bunch of wire together in the right way, you can make that magnet stronger.[2]

You probably have some magnets on your refrigerator, and those don't have any current running through them, so why are they magnets? The magnet is matter, and what makes up matter? Atoms. And you know an atom is a positive nucleus surrounded by whirling negative electrons. And "whirling" is a kind of motion, so every atom contains tiny moving charges. All of those currents act like incredibly small magnets.

In most materials, those little whirling charges are going in all different directions. In some materials, though, the currents line up. That turns some types of matter into magnets. Explaining why those currents line up is very complicated, but it ends up being an explanation you have already seen: in certain materials, those currents line up when they are in equilibrium.

Physics in Your Everyday Life

Electricity and Magnetism Together

The gravitational attraction of Earth pulls everything toward Earth's center. But gravity also pulls in all the places where there isn't any object. You can think of this as if Earth fills all of space with a gravitational field. Any object in that field will feel Earth's pull.

Electricity and magnetism are similar. Electric charge creates an electric field. Moving electric charge creates a magnetic field. The fields are there even if there is not another electric charge and even if there is not a piece of iron nearby.

This ends up being really important because it turns out that a changing electric field can create a magnetic field, and a changing magnetic field can create an electric field. If that were not true, then, for example, electric and magnetic fields could not work together to make light.

Electricity and Magnetism

MAGNETIC FIELD

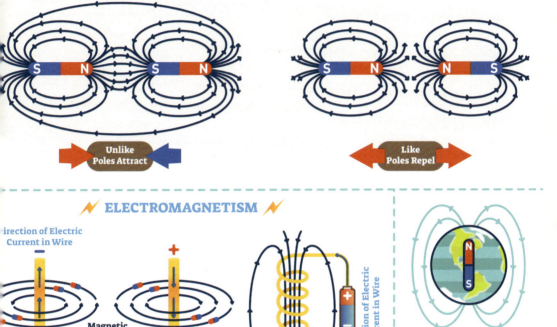

Electricity and magnetism are connected together in interesting ways. Electricity is around anytime there are charged particles, and magnetism appears anytime those charged particles are moving.

55

Activity: Static Electricity

After two balloons have been rubbed against a cloth, they can stick to a wall. They also push each other away. That's electrical charge in action!

Things You Will Need:

- 2 balloons
- a fleece blanket or fleece clothing

Electricity and Magnetism

■ **1.** Blow up the balloons.

■ **2.** Hold them by the knots so they hang down. Bring them close together while they're hanging down.

■ **3.** Now rub them both against the fleece for about thirty seconds and hold them hanging by the knots again.

■ **4.** Bring them close, making sure the sides you rubbed are facing each other. What is different about how they act?

When you rub the balloon on the fleece, you transfer charge between balloon and fleece. You can't see it, but you can see its effects. You treat identical balloons the same way, so they end up with similar charge. That's why they repel one another.

You may also notice the balloons are attracted to you—you may feel the hairs on your arms rise as the balloons are nearby. That's a little more complicated to explain, except for one thing: your hair and the balloon attract one another because they are oppositely charged.

Afterword

Physics is the study of energy and matter. Since everything in the universe is either energy or matter, physics is the study of everything in the universe. But remember, the things you discover in your kitchen are true everywhere in the universe.

The demonstrations you have done have given you some idea about how observations can provide clues into how the universe works. You can test your own ideas about how the universe works. When you have an idea, think about a test you could perform that would show if your idea were true. If your test comes out the way you thought, that's a hint your idea might be true.

Those kinds of tests are called experiments, and when you do your own, you are taking the same path that physicists and other scientists are traveling. So try some of your own. Maybe you can spin a can of soup and a can of pumpkin and see how they act differently. What happens if you submerge a spoon handle in a half glass of water? Can you sing a note that vibrates the walls in your bathroom? You can safely make very interesting experiments with things you already have in your house.

Physics is the study of the universe, and the universe is all around you, including in your own home. Explore your home and you explore the universe!

Chapter Notes

■ Chapter 1
The Rules of the World
1. Abel B. Franco, "Avempace, Projectile Motion, and Impetus Theory," *Journal of the History of Ideas* 64, no. 4 (October 2003): pp. 521–546, doi:10.1353/jhi.2004.0004.

■ Chapter 2
Learning from Motion
1. The NEED Project, "Introduction to Energy," National Science Digital Library, 2017, http://nsdl.oercommons.org/courses/introduction-to-energy-3/view.

■ Chapter 4
Sound
1. Tom Henderson, "The Anatomy of a Wave," The Physics Classroom, accessed October 20, 2018, https://www.physicsclassroom.com/class/waves/Lesson-2/The-Anatomy-of-a-Wave.
2. "Speed of Sound," NASA, updated March 23, 2018, https://www.grc.nasa.gov/www/k-12/airplane/sound.html.

■ Chapter 6
Electricity and Magnetism
1. "Triboelectric Effect," Harvard University, accessed October 27, 2018, https://sciencedemonstrations.fas.harvard.edu/presentations/triboelectric-effects.
2. Teach Engineering/Vanderbilt University, "Building an Electromagnet," National Science Digital Library, accessed October 27, 2018, https://nsdl.oercommons.org/courses/building-an-electromagnet-3/view.

atom A small piece of matter consisting of a relatively heavy positive nucleus surrounded by light, whirling electrons.

charge A property of matter. There are two types of charge: positive and negative. Similar charges repel each other, while opposite charges attract.

controlled experiment A test of one aspect of an event, keeping other things constant.

electricity A description of things that happen due to the presence of electric charge, whether still or moving.

electron A negatively charged particle whirling around the nucleus of an atom.

equilibrium Balance, especially referring to a point where different forces are balanced.

impetus An initial surge given to a body to get it moving. It was thought that the body would stop moving when the impetus ran out.

magnetism A property of some matter, created by moving charge of one sort or another, that enables it to attract iron and certain other materials.

mass A property of an object that describes how much it resists motion. Very similar to weight, we would say a heavy object is harder to move than a light one.

net force The total of all the forces acting on an object. Even with many forces around, the net force can still add to zero.

neutron A particle in the nucleus of an atom, about two thousand times the mass of an electron. The neutron has no electric charge.

Glossary

proton A positively charged particle in the nucleus of an atom. Like the neutron, a proton is about two thousand times the mass of an electron.

resonant frequency The rate at which a system vibrates when it is nudged away from equilibrium. It is also the rate at which a system most easily transfers energy in and out.

restoring force A force that acts to return an object to its equilibrium position.

simple harmonic motion The motion of an object when a simple restoring force pushes or pulls it back to its equilibrium position, perhaps its "starting point."

theory A model of some aspect of the universe that accounts for observations and makes predictions about unobserved phenomena.

Books

Bloomfield, Louis. *How Things Work: The Physics of Everyday Life.* New York, NY: John Wiley & Sons, 2016.

Gray, Theodore. *Molecules: The Elements and the Architecture of Everything.* New York, NY: Black Dog & Leventhal Publishers, 2018.

Kakalios, James. *The Physics of Everyday Things.* New York, NY: Crown Publishing, 2017.

Mercer, Bobby. *Junk Drawer Physics: 50 Awesome Experiments That Don't Cost a Thing.* Chicago, IL: Chicago Review Press, 2014.

Petersen, Kristen. *Understanding Forces of Nature: Gravity, Electricity, and Magnetism.* New York, NY: Cavendish Square, 2015.

VanCleave, Janice Pratt. *More of Janice VanCleave's Wild, Wacky, and Weird Physics Experiments.* New York, NY: Rosen Central, 2017.

Websites

APS PhysicsCentral
www.physicscentral.org

Watch demonstrations, read articles on current research, and get to know people who work in physics.

The Physics Classroom
www.physicsclassroom.com

Find more in-depth information and experiments on different physics topics.

The Universe Adventure
www.universeadventure.org

Explore what makes up the universe, how it came to be, and current theories and research.

Index

A
Aristotle, 9–11, 14
atoms, 25–27, 33, 40–42, 53

B
biologists, 6

C
chemists, 6
compression, 37

D
density, 34–35

E
electricity, 49, 51–52, 54
    electric charge, 49–50, 56
    electric current, 52–53
    electric field, 44
electromagnetism, 55
electrons, 25–26, 53
energy, 6, 21, 33, 37, 40–41, 43
    kinetic energy, 21
    law of conservation of energy, 22
    potential energy (energy of position), 22
equilibrium, 19, 34, 43–44, 53

evidence, 7
experiment, 14, 58
    controlled, 16

F
force, 11, 17–18, 26–27, 33, 35
    net force, 17, 26, 49–50
    restoring force, 19, 20, 34, 43
frequency, 35
    natural frequency (resonant frequency), 41–42
friction, 42

G
gas, 27–30
gravitational attraction, 19, 54
gravity, 19, 49–50, 54

I
impetus, 11

K
kinetic energy, 21

L
liquid, 27–30

63

Physics in Your Everyday Life

M

magnetic field, 44, 54–55
magnetism, 44, 54–55, 51
mass, 21
matter, 6, 25, 27, 33, 53
molecules, 25–27, 33, 35, 40, 45–46
motion, 29

N

natural frequency (resonant frequency), 41–42
neutrons, 25–26
Newton, Issac 11–14, 17
    laws of motion, 13, 17, 49
nucleus, 25–26, 51, 53

O

observation, 7, 24, 50–52, 58

P

particles, 34
Philoponus, John , 11, 14
photoreceptor cells, 45
physicist, 7, 58
physics, 6
potential energy (energy of position), 22
pressure, 27, 31, 35
pressure wave, 36
protons, 25–26, 51

R

rarefaction, 37

retina, 45

S

simple harmonic motion, 19, 25–26, 39
solid, 27–30
sound waves, 34–39

T

temperature, 29, 31–32
theory, 7, 59

V

vibration, 36–38, 43